The Northeast

DANA MEACHEN RAU

Children's Press®
An Imprint of Scholastic Inc.
New York Toronto London Auckland Sydney
Mexico City New Delhi Hong Kong
Danbury, Connecticut

Front cover, center: Brooklyn Bridge in New York City, New York
Front cover, top right: Moose Pond near Mount Pleasant in Maine
Front cover, bottom left: Old State House in Boston, Massachusetts

Content Consultant
James Wolfinger, PhD
Associate Professor
DePaul University
Chicago, Illinois

Library of Congress Cataloging-in-Publication Data

Rau, Dana Meachen, 1971–
 The Northeast/by Dana Meachen Rau.
   p. cm.—(A true book)
 Includes bibliographical references and index.
  ISBN-13: 978-0-531-24851-5 (lib. bdg.)   ISBN-10: 0-531-24851-8 (lib. bdg.)
  ISBN-13: 978-0-531-28326-4 (pbk.)   ISBN-10: 0-531-28326-7 (pbk.)
  1. Northeastern States—Juvenile literature. 2. Middle Atlantic
States—Juvenile literature. I. Title. II. Series.
 F4.3.R38 2012
 974—dc23   2011031706

All rights reserved. Published in 2012 by Children's Press, an imprint of Scholastic Inc.
Printed in China 62
SCHOLASTIC, CHILDREN'S PRESS, A TRUE BOOK, and associated logos are trademarks and/or registered trademarks of Scholastic Inc.
1 2 3 4 5 6 7 8 9 10 R 21 20 19 18 17 16 15 14 13 12

Find the Truth!

Everything you are about to read is true *except* for one of the sentences on this page.

Which one is **TRUE**?

T or F   New York City is the most populated city in the United States.

T or F   The Massachusetts Bay Colony was the only English settlement in America.

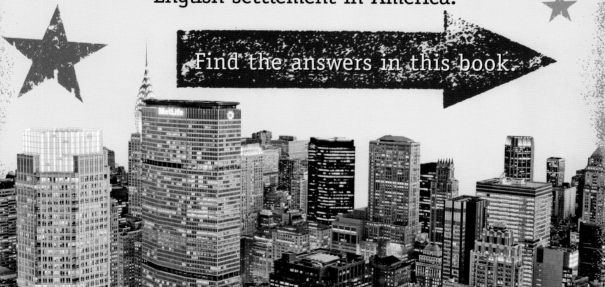

Find the answers in this book.

Contents

THE **BIG** TRUTH!

Animals of the Northeast

Eastern bluebird

Times Square in
New York City

4 Resources and Economy

How does the Northeast make use of its
resources? **31**

5 Bringing Back the Cities

What challenges does the Northeast face? **39**

Rivers provided
Native Americans
with food and
travel routes.

5

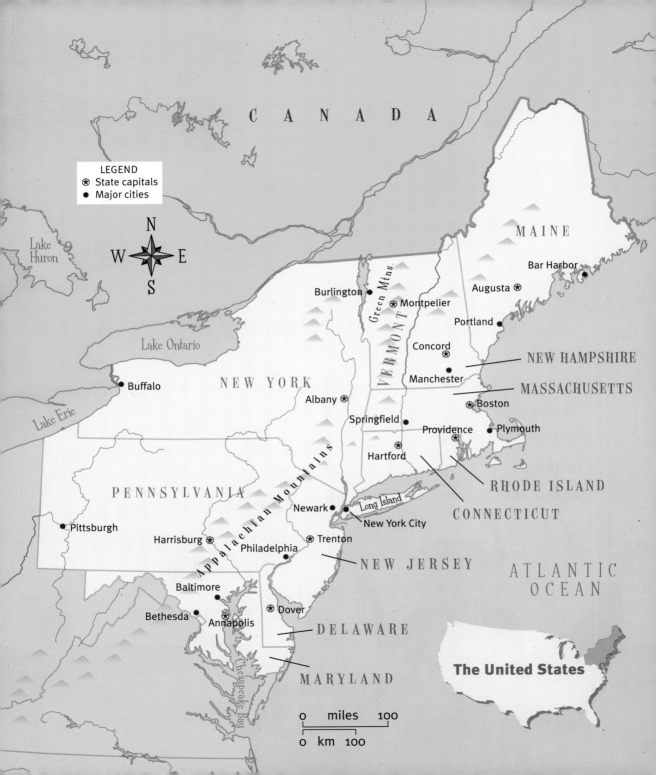

C A N A D A

LEGEND
⊛ State capitals
● Major cities

Lake
Huron

Lake Ontario

Lake Erie

N
W E
S

MAINE

Bar Harbor ●

Burlington ●
Augusta ⊛

⊛ Montpelier

Portland ●

Green Mtns.

Concord ⊛

NEW HAMPSHIRE

NEW YORK

VERMONT

Manchester ●

MASSACHUSETTS

Buffalo ●

Albany ⊛

⊛ Boston

Springfield ●

Providence ⊛ ● Plymouth

Hartford ⊛

RHODE ISLAND

Long Island

CONNECTICUT

PENNSYLVANIA

Newark ●

New York City

Pittsburgh ●

Appalachian Mountains

Harrisburg ⊛

Trenton ⊛

Philadelphia ●

NEW JERSEY

ATLANTIC
OCEAN

Baltimore ●

Bethesda ●

Dover ⊛

⊛ Annapolis

DELAWARE

The United States

Chesapeake Bay

MARYLAND

0   miles   100

0   km   100

CHAPTER 1

High Mountains and Stormy Seas

The Northeast region includes 11 states. The states are Connecticut, Delaware, Maine, Maryland, Massachusetts, New Hampshire, New Jersey, New York, Pennsylvania, Rhode Island, and Vermont. New England is another name for the six states farthest north. People sometimes call the other five states in this region the Mid-Atlantic states. The Northeast shares a border with Canada in the north and the southeastern states in the south.

The Appalachian Mountains stretch 1,500 miles (2,400 kilometers).

Look at the Land

The Northeast has a long coastline along the Atlantic Ocean. In the northern coastal areas, lighthouses warn sailors away from the rocky coast. Farther south, the coast has sandy beaches.

Scattered near the coast are several small islands, such as Martha's Vineyard and Block Island. These islands are busiest in summer, when the weather is warm enough for **tourists** to visit the many beaches there. Other islands are quite large, such as Long Island and Manhattan.

The beaches along the Atlantic coast draw large crowds during the hot summer months.

New York's Coney Island has been a popular vacation spot since the 1800s.

The Appalachian Trail is popular with hikers.

The Appalachian Mountain range stretches from Canada to Alabama. It once formed a natural border between the settled parts of the east and the unexplored western areas.

Many rivers run through the region. They cut through the rich soil of the coastal plain and flow into the ocean. Native Americans, settlers, and industries have all used these waterways as routes for travel and to deliver goods.

Rakes help keep snow from damaging roofs.

Heavy winter snowstorms are common in many parts of the Northeast.

Climate

Most of the Northeast has a humid **continental climate**. Summers are warm, and winters are cold. Spring and autumn are mild. **Precipitation** falls throughout the year as rain in the summer and snow in the winter. Some northern parts of the region are covered in snow during the entire winter season. The lower northeastern states have a humid subtropical climate. Their winters are not as cold as the winters up north.

Stormy Weather

Nor'easters are severe storms that often hit the region between October and April. These storms form over the Atlantic Ocean. Northeast winds blow the storm up the east coast of the United States. Nor'easters have strong winds. Their waves erode the land on the coasts. Large amounts of rain and snow may cause flooding.

It is possible for hurricanes to make their way up the eastern coastline. In 2011, Hurricane Irene caused severe flooding and damage to the Northeast region. Homes and businesses were ruined, and people were without power for many days.

Hurricane Irene caused major flooding as far north as the border between the United States and Canada.

Valuable Forests

The climate of the region is ideal for forests to grow. Some trees, such as white pines and hemlocks, have thin needlelike leaves and grow pinecones. The white pine is both the state tree and state flower of Maine.

The forests have long provided people with animals for food, wood for shelter, and other resources. Sap from maple trees even provides a sweet treat when made into maple syrup.

Maple sap is collected by drilling holes into trees and letting the sap drip into buckets.

Mountain laurel is the state flower of Connecticut and Pennsylvania.

Mountain laurel is one of the many wildflowers to bloom in the Northeast during the summer.

Change of Seasons

The changing temperatures and weather create four distinct seasons. These seasons trigger changes to the northeastern landscape's color. Forests and fields burst with green leaves in spring. Flowers bloom with purple and pink blossoms in summer. Oak and maple trees light up with red, yellow, and orange **foliage** in autumn. Winter brings white blankets of snow.

Native Americans in the Northeast often fished from their canoes.

History of the Northeast

The word *new* pops up a lot in Northeastern region names. Just think of New England, New York, New Hampshire, and New Jersey. This area was new to settlers from Europe. But many Native Americans had been living in the Northeast for thousands of years. The Algonquin and the Iroquois were two of the main groups. The tribes used the region's trees to build shelters and canoes. The land and sea provided food.

Native American canoes were made from tree bark.

Explorers and Settlers

Europeans from England, France, Sweden, and Holland started exploring the region in the late 1500s and early 1600s. Then settlers arrived to form **colonies**. In 1620, a group from England settled in present-day Massachusetts and formed the Plymouth Colony. More English settlers formed the Massachusetts Bay Colony in 1628.

The early settlers of Plymouth worked together to build homes and create a new community.

Only half of the Plymouth settlers survived their first harsh winter.

16

The new settlers found plenty of wood to use for construction.

Colonies expanded to today's Connecticut, Rhode Island, New Hampshire, and Pennsylvania. The Dutch settled parts of present-day New York. The Dutch and Swedes settled in what is now New Jersey. The fertile land helped farming become central to many communities. Other colonies near the ocean relied on fishing. Those with forests used the lumber for building.

Fight for Freedom

England and France argued over who owned the land in America. They fought the French and Indian War from 1754 to 1763. France and its native **allies** fought against England for control of the region. England won.

The king of England, on the other side of the Atlantic Ocean, ruled over the colonies. The colonies wanted to be independent. They worked together to fight against the British.

Northeastern Timeline

1524
Giovanni da Verrazano, exploring for France, sails along the northeastern coast.

1620
Pilgrims start a colony in Plymouth, Massachusetts.

The colonists were not expert soldiers like the British. But they knew the forests, rivers, and landscapes of their region well. The British relied on more formal methods of battle. The colonists, however, used their knowledge of the land to their advantage. The colonists won. America became a free country. The colonies became states. They called themselves the United States of America.

1775–1783

Colonists fight against England in the Revolutionary War.

1754–1763

England and France fight in the French and Indian War.

1820

New York becomes the main port of entry for immigrants.

A Growing Nation

The United States grew as a nation. Cities became centers of trade. Newly built railroads and canals connecting natural waterways helped join the country together.

Just like the early settlers, people continued to come to America from other countries. From the early 1800s to the early 1900s, millions of European **immigrants** arrived in northeastern ports looking for a new life in America.

Most immigrants to the Northeast entered the United States through Ellis Island, in New York Harbor.

Artists and Inventors of the Northeast

Dr. Seuss (1904–1991) is one of the most popular children's book authors of all time. He was born in Massachusetts as Theodor Seuss Geisel.

Dr. Suess

Phineas Taylor Barnum (1810–1891) was a showman who founded a circus he called The Greatest Show on Earth. He was born in Connecticut.

Samuel F. B. Morse (1791–1872) was the inventor of the electric telegraph, the developer of the Morse code, and an artist. He was born in Massachusetts.

Norman Rockwell (1894–1978) was one of the best-known U.S. painters and illustrators of the 20th century. He was born in New York City.

Northeastern cities such as Baltimore, Maryland, are home to people from a wide variety of backgrounds.

CHAPTER 3

People of the Northeast

Immigrants poured into the northeastern cities in the 1800s. Some stayed to work in the cities' industries. Others left to explore, settle, or farm the land. All of them brought the culture and traditions of their countries to their new homes in the United States. That's why America is often called a melting pot. Today, the population of the Northeast is still made up of people with many different backgrounds. This is especially true in cities.

The Biggest City

New York City is the largest city in the United States. Its **diverse** population includes people from around the world. Sights, sounds, smells, and traditions of different cultures surround visitors. Many new immigrants settle near people who came from the same country. That way, they can speak their native languages and practice familiar traditions. In some neighborhoods, many residents speak Spanish. Chinatown resembles streets in China, with markets selling traditional foods.

Times Square in New York City is busy both day and night.

24

New York City has more than 26,000 people per square mile.

Much of New York City is located on three small islands. The limited space affects how people live and work. Buildings with apartments and offices stretch up instead of outward. These are called skyscrapers. Some New Yorkers live outside the city center where there is a little more space. Many of them travel to work by train. Others take ferries that go between the islands and the mainland. Some drive across bridges such as the Brooklyn Bridge.

The Northeast is known for small towns such as Bar Harbor, Maine.

Town and Country

Maine, New Hampshire, Vermont, and upper New York are the region's most rural areas. Populations there are much smaller. Some people work on farms, where they grow fruits or vegetables or raise dairy cows. Many people own or work at small businesses that serve the community. Grocery stores, farm equipment suppliers, and clothing stores provide residents goods as well as employment. Some grocery stores specialize in selling foods grown on local farms.

Celebrating Traditions

Amish people live in Lancaster County, Pennsylvania. They are related to Swiss and German settlers of the early 1700s. They still hold on to traditional ways, such as riding horses instead of using cars and wearing simple clothing.

Marylanders practice a very old tradition as their state sport: **jousting**. Early English colonists brought the sport over in the 1600s. Residents have jousted ever since. Today, men and women of all ages take part in tournaments, though they no longer use the traditional, sharp lances when they play.

About 30,000 Amish people live in Lancaster County.

Animals of the Northeast

Many animals live on the land, in the waters, and in the skies of the Northeast.

Eastern bluebirds live in open areas near trees. They feed on insects and berries. Fewer bluebirds live in the Northeast now than in the past. People are trying to bring them back. They set up special bluebird boxes where the birds can build their nests.

Northern lobsters live along the rocky bottom of the ocean. They have thick, hard shells. They use their claws to crush and tear apart food.

Moose are excellent swimmers. In the summer, they eat plants that grow in shallow water. They can dive to reach deeper water plants. During winter, they often survive on pinecones, bark, and shrubs.

Eastern gray squirrels collect nuts and scurry up trees in parks, forests, and backyards. Their bushy tails shield them from rain and sun. Their tails also keep them warm in the winter.

Sailing is a popular pasttime in the Northeast.

CHAPTER 4

Resources and Economy

The natural beauty of the changing northeastern seasons attracts tourists. Many people come to the region to ski in the White Mountains of New Hampshire or the Green Mountains of Vermont. Others visit beaches along the Atlantic to swim or sail. Some tourists drive through small New England towns to get a glimpse of the bright fall foliage. The tourist industry provides jobs for residents in restaurants and hotels that serve visitors.

 Marinas are like parking lots for boats.

Ocean Opportunities

The Northeast's extensive ocean border plays an important part in the fishing industry. Maine fishers catch fresh lobsters. Fishing boats bring in scallops from the coast of Massachusetts. Chesapeake Bay produces blue crabs. Rhode Islanders catch flounder and squid. People protect these valuable resources by preventing overfishing and reducing pollution in the ocean.

Commercial fishers use huge nets to catch many fish at once.

Cranes unload heavy containers at the Port of New York.

Ports are busy coastal areas where ships load and unload cargo. They are often in deep water that can accommodate large ships. The Northeast is home to many ports that support the economy of the entire United States. Baltimore, New York City, and Philadelphia are major U.S. ports where goods arrive from other countries. U.S. goods are also shipped out to the world.

The average U.S. dairy farm has 115 cows.

Dairy cows spend much of their time eating grass in large fields of green grass.

Farming

The rich soil of the river valleys and coastal plains is excellent for growing crops. Some farmers grow vegetables, such as bell peppers in New Jersey and mushrooms in Pennsylvania. Fruits, such as apples and grapes, grow well in New York. Wild blueberries grow in Maine.

Dairy farms are found throughout the Northeast. Cows graze in the region's grassy fields. Milk from these farms is used to make ice cream, cheese, yogurt, and other dairy products.

Mining

Northeasterners also benefit from underground resources. Pennsylvania is one of the leading coal-mining states. Coal is used to create electricity and to fuel steel mills.

During the 1800s, Pittsburgh, Pennsylvania, became known as the Steel City. It produced the iron and steel to build the railroads, bridges, and machinery of the growing United States. Today, Pittsburgh steel is still important. The city produces special steel used for planes, power plants, and high-tech electronics.

At a mill in Pittsburgh, Pennsylvania, metal is heated so it can be molded into different shapes.

Industries

Wall Street in New York City is a center of **finance**. Many major businesses, banks, and other organizations are based here. These groups deal with money-related activities, such as bank loans and selling or buying **stocks**.

The health industry is important in Massachusetts. Boston has some of the nation's best hospitals. Doctors and medical students from many countries come here to work and study. They research new treatments for cancer, heart disease, and other health issues.

Many of the country's best doctors work at Children's Hospital Boston.

Shooting Hoops

The first game of
basketball was
played in 1891
in Springfield,
Massachusetts.
James Naismith
was a physical
education
teacher in
Springfield. He made

up a new game for his players. They tossed a
soccer ball into peach baskets.

Basketball has become a major college,
professional, and Olympic sport for both men and
women. It's very popular with kids, too! Today,
people visit the Naismith Memorial Basketball Hall
of Fame in Springfield. It was built in the shape of
a basketball.

Northeastern mills once made cloth that was sold and shipped around the world.

CHAPTER 5

Bringing Back the Cities

Throughout history, the cities of the Northeast were booming centers of industry. But during the second half of the 1900s, these industries began to shut down. One reason that U.S. factories closed is that many products could be made more cheaply in other countries. Thousands of workers lost their jobs. People moved away to look for work.

Factory and apartment buildings sat empty. Stores, restaurants, and other businesses closed because they did not have enough customers. Cities had to find a way to bring people and businesses back.

A Better Future

Citizens and governments looked for ways to improve things. State and U.S. governments passed laws to clean up pollution left behind by the old factories. Cleaner air and water made the cities more attractive to new residents.

Local governments improved roads, tunnels, and public transportation systems. People and goods could travel into or out of the cities more easily. This encouraged companies to locate their offices, factories, or stores there. This created more jobs.

Many cities had become run down by the 1960s.

Many industrial buildings in northeastern cities have been turned into apartments.

More recently, cities are reusing their buildings and other resources. Abandoned factories and apartment buildings are becoming new offices, apartments, or places for people to gather. Cities such as Bethesda, Maryland, are turning unused areas into shopping centers that support local and national companies. Old railroad tracks are becoming sidewalks and trails. This is creating more green, open spaces within a city, without clearing forests or taking over farmland.

Nearly 50 million people visit New York City each year.

Southeastern Pennsylvania and other areas are working on improving their public transportation. They are developing new buses and trains that create less pollution. New train and bus routes are also being introduced. This makes travel through and between cities easier.

As these programs help the region's cities and rural areas to grow, Northeasterners will continue to use and enjoy the many resources the region has to offer. ★

Number of states in the region: 11

Major rivers of the region: Connecticut, Hudson, Delaware

Major mountain range of the region: Appalachian

Climates: Humid continental and humid subtropical

Largest cities: New York, NY; Philadelphia, PA; Baltimore, MD

Products: Fish, fruits, vegetables, stone, lumber, coal

Borders of the region:

North: Canada

East: Atlantic Ocean

South: Southeast region

West: Midwest region

Did you find the truth?

(T) New York City is the most populated city in the United States.

(F) The Massachusetts Bay Colony was the only English settlement in America.

Resources

Books

Harmon, Daniel E. *The Hudson River*. Philadelphia: Chelsea House Publishers, 2004.

Mattern, Joanne. *New York City*. Edina, MN: Abdo Publishing Co., 2007.

Maynard, Charles W. *The Appalachians*. New York: PowerKids Press, 2004.

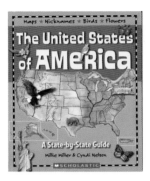

Miller, Millie, and Cyndi Nelson. *The United States of America: A State-by-State Guide*. New York: Scholastic Reference, 2006.

Rau, Dana Meachen. *North America*. Chanhassen, MN: The Child's World, 2004.

Rosinsky, Natalie Myra. *The Wampanoag and Their History*. Minneapolis: Compass Point Books, 2005.

Shea, Kitty Patricia. *Industrial America*. Minneapolis: Compass Point Books, 2005.

Waxman, Laura Hamilton. *Why Did the Pilgrims Come to the New World?* Minneapolis: Lerner Publications, 2011.

Web Sites

Smithsonian National Museum of American History
http://americanhistory.si.edu
Check out this site to see exhibits and learn about the growth of America.

U.S. Census 2010 — Interactive Population Map
http://2010.census.gov/2010census/popmap/
Learn about the populations of the states with this interactive map.

Places to Visit

Mystic Seaport: The Museum of America and the Sea
75 Greenmanville Avenue
Mystic, CT 06355
(860) 572-0711
www.mysticseaport.org
Once a center of shipbuilding, this seaport now holds maritime artifacts, ships to tour, and historical houses.

Statue of Liberty National Monument and Ellis Island
Liberty Island
New York, NY 10004-1467
(212) 363-3200
www.nps.gov/elis/index.htm
Visit the Ellis Island Immigration Museum to see exhibits on American immigrants and view the statue that greeted them.

Visit this Scholastic web site for more information on the U.S. Northeast:
www.factsfornow.scholastic.com

Important Words

allies (AL-eyez) — people, countries, or groups that are on the same side during a war or disagreement

colonies (KOL-uh-neez) — territories that have been settled by people from another country and are controlled by that country

continental climate (kon-tuh-NEN-tuhl KLYE-mit) — the weather typical of a place that has yearly temperature variations between winter and summer

diverse (dih-VURS) — having many different types or kinds

finance (FYE-nans) — the management and use of money by businesses, banks, and governments

foliage (FOH-lee-ij) — leaves of a plant or tree

jousting (JOWST-ing) —taking part in a competition between two people on horseback with lances

immigrants (IM-i-gruhntz) — people who move into a new country and settle there

precipitation (pri-sip-i-TAY-shuhn) — the falling of water from the sky in the form of rain, sleet, hail, or snow

stocks (STAHKS) — if you own stock in a company, you have invested money in it and own part of the company

tourists (TOOR-ists) — people who travel and visit places for pleasure

Index

Page numbers in **bold** indicate illustrations

About the Author

Dana Meachen Rau is the author of more than 300 books for children. A graduate of Trinity College in Hartford, Connecticut, she has written fiction and nonfiction titles including early readers and books on science, history, cooking, and many other topics that interest her. She especially loves to write books that take her to other places, even when she doesn't have time for a vacation. Dana lives with her family in Burlington, Connecticut. To learn more about her books, please visit *www.danameachenrau.com*.